DIALYSIS COOKBOOK

40+ Side Dishes, salad and pasta recipes designed for Dialysis

TABLE OF CONTENTS

publisher.

Introduction

Dialysis recipes for personal enjoyment but also for family enjoyment. You will love them for sure for how easy it is to prepare them.

VEGGIE BURGERS

Serves:	**4**	
Prep Time:	**5**	Minutes
Cook Time:	**15**	Minutes
Total Time:	**20**	Minutes

INGREDIENTS

- 1 lb. beef
- 1 carrot
- 1 zucchini
- 3 cloves garlic
- ¼ cup parsley
- 1 tablespoon parmesan
- 1 tablespoon coconut oil

DIRECTIONS

1. Grate zucchini and carrots in a bowl
2. In a pan melt coconut oil, add garlic, carrots, parsley, zucchini, pepper, salt and sauté for 2-3 minutes
3. Combine vegetables with beef, parmesan, mix and form patties
4. Grill the patties for 3-4 minutes per side
5. When ready remove and serve

Serves: **6**

Prep Time: **5**   Minutes

Cook Time: **20** Minutes

Total Time: **25** Minutes

INGREDIENTS

- 5 carrots
- 1 cup water
- 2 tablespoons sugar
- 1 tablespoon butter
- 1 tablespoon lemon juice

DIRECTIONS

1. In a saucepan bring carrots to a boil
2. Simmer for 5-10 minutes
3. Add remaining ingredients and simmer for another 5-10 minutes
4. When ready remove and serve

Serves: *4*

Prep Time: *5* Minutes

Cook Time: *15* Minutes

Total Time: *20* Minutes

INGREDIENTS

- 4 salmon fillets
- 2 tablespoons olive oil
- 1 tsp salt

DIRECTIONS

1. Pat dry salmon fillets and sprinkle with salt and olive oil
2. Place in oven on the top rack and broil for 12-15 minutes
3. When done, add sliced lemon and serve

Serves: **4**

Prep Time: **5**   Minutes

Cook Time: **10** Minutes

Total Time: **15** Minutes

INGREDIENTS

- 1 lb. asparagus
- 1 tablespoon olive oil
- 2 garlic cloves
- 2 tablespoons parmesan
- Juice of 1 lemon

DIRECTIONS

1. On a baking sheet arrange the asparagus and toss in the olive oil
2. Sprinkle with salt and pepper
3. Roast for 10-12 minutes or until tender
4. Toss in garlic, parmesan and lemon juice
5. When ready remove and serve

Serves: *4*

Prep Time: *5*   Minutes

Cook Time: *20* Minutes

Total Time: *25* Minutes

INGREDIENTS

- 4 cups water
- 1 sheet nori
- 1 tsp grated ginger
- 4 tablespoons miso paste
- ½ cup green onion
- 2 baby bok choys
- 1 cup shiitake mushrooms
- ½ cup tofu
- Salt

DIRECTIONS

1. Bring water to a simmer
2. Add in nori and simmer for another 4-5 minutes
3. In another bowl add ½ cup water, miso paste and stir until miso dissolves completely

4. Add ginger, onion, bok choy, tofu, mushrooms, and simmer for 10-12 minutes

5. Remove pot from heat and stir in miso mixture

6. Stir well and taste

7. When ready pour into bowls and serve

Serves: **2**

Prep Time: **5** Minutes

Cook Time: **5** Minutes

Total Time: **10** Minutes

INGREDIENTS

- 2 tablespoons water
- 1 tablespoon olive oil
- 1 tablespoon lemon juice
- ¼ cup parsley leaves
- ½ tsp hot sauce
- 1 garlic clove
- ½ cup green soybeans

DIRECTIONS

1. In a blender combine all ingredients together and blend until smooth
2. Cover and let it stand
3. When ready serve with tortilla chips

Serves: **4**

Prep Time: **5**   Minutes

Cook Time: **20**   Minutes

Total Time: **25**   Minutes

INGREDIENTS

- 1 lb. white fish
- 1 tsp onion
- ¼ tsp mustard
- ¼ tsp dill weed
- Pepper
- 2 tablespoon lemon juice

DIRECTIONS

1. Rinse fish and pat it dry
2. Place in a baking dish and add the rest of ingredients
3. Bake at 450 F for 18-20 minutes
4. When ready remove and serve

Serves: **6**

Prep Time: **5** Minutes

Cook Time: **10** Minutes

Total Time: **15** Minutes

INGREDIENTS

- 1 tablespoon carrots
- 1 cup white vinegar
- ¼ cup rice vinegar
- 1 tablespoon sugar
- ½ tsp pepper
- 1 tsp garlic powder

DIRECTIONS

1. Cut the carrots and steam in the microwave for 4-5 minutes
2. In another bowl combine all ingredients together
3. Pour mixture over carrots and serve

Serves: **4**

Prep Time: **10** Minutes

Cook Time: **30** Minutes

Total Time: **40** Minutes

INGREDIENTS

- 2 chicken breasts
- ¼ cup mustard
- 2 tablespoons honey
- 1 tsp lemon juice
- 1 tsp curry powder

DIRECTIONS

1. Place chicken in a baking dish
2. In another bowl combine the rest of ingredients
3. Brush both sides of chicken breast
4. Bake for 25-30 minutes at 325 F
5. When ready remove and serve

Serves: **2**

Prep Time: **5**   Minutes

Cook Time: **5**   Minutes

Total Time: **10** Minutes

INGREDIENTS

- ½ cup mayonnaise
- 1 tablespoon vinegar
- 1 cup shell macaroni
- 1 can unsalted tuna
- ¼ cup peas
- ¼ celery
- 1 tablespoon dill weed

DIRECTIONS

1. In a bowl combine all ingredients together
2. Cover and chill
3. Serve when ready

Serves: **6**

Prep Time: **15** Minutes

Cook Time: **45** Minutes

Total Time: **60** Minutes

INGREDIENTS

- 4 beets
- 1 tsp salt
- 1 tablespoon olive oil
- 1 tablespoon maple syrup

DIRECTIONS

1. Cut the beets in 1-inch cubes
2. Place the beets on a baking sheet and toss with salt and olive oil
3. Roast for 30-40 minutes at 375 F
4. In a pan add maple syrup, vinegar and cook until liquid is evaporated
5. Toss the glaze with the roasted beets and serve

Serves: **4**

Prep Time: **5** Minutes

Cook Time: **20** Minutes

Total Time: **25** Minutes

INGREDIENTS

- 1 tsp olive oil
- ¼ onion
- 1 tsp garlic
- 1 bunch collard greens
- ¼ tsp black pepper
- ¼ tsp red pepper flakes
- 1 cup chicken broth
- 1 tablespoon vinegar

DIRECTIONS

1. In a saucepan heat oil and add garlic and onions
2. Add greens, onion and remaining ingredients
3. Reduce heat and simmer for 15-20 minutes or until tender
4. When ready remove and serve

Serves: 2

Prep Time: 5   Minutes

Cook Time: 5   Minutes

Total Time: 10   Minutes

INGREDIENTS

- 1 cup cooked chicken
- ¼ cup celery
- ¼ cup green pepper
- ¼ cup onion
- 1 cup oranges
- ¼ cup mayonnaise

DIRECTIONS

1. In a bowl combine onion, green pepper and mayonnaise
2. Toss chicken, green pepper, and celery with mayonnaise mixture
3. On a bread slice add orange slices, chicken and the rest of ingredients
4. Serve when ready

Serves: *1*
Prep Time: *5*   Minutes

Cook Time: *5*   Minutes

Total Time: *10* Minutes

INGREDIENTS

- 8 chicken drumsticks
- 1 tablespoon olive oil
- 1 tsp salt
- 1 tsp garlic
- 1 onion
- 1lb. figs
- 1 tablespoon chives

DIRECTIONS

1. Place drumsticks in a baking dish and drizzle olive oil, garlic powder, salt and bake for 90 minutes at 350 F
2. In the last 15-20 minutes, add onion, olive oil to a saucepan and cook until tender
3. Add balsamic vinegar, figs, salt, and chopped chives

4. When the drumsticks are done, remove and spoon the of the fig sauce over the drumsticks

Serves: **2**

Prep Time: **5**   Minutes

Cook Time: **10**   Minutes

Total Time: **15**   Minutes

INGREDIENTS

- 1 tsp olive oil
- ¼ red bell pepper
- 4 green onions
- 4 eggs
- 2 corn tortillas

DIRECTIONS

1. In a frying pan add green onion, bell pepper and cook for 3-4 minutes
2. Add eggs and scramble for 2-3 minutes
3. On a tortilla wrap spoon egg mixture and roll
4. Serve when ready

Serves: **6**

Prep Time: **10**   Minutes

Cook Time: **60**   Minutes

Total Time: **70**   Minutes

INGREDIENTS

- 1 onion
- 2 chicken breasts
- 2 tablespoons unsalted butter
- 2 eggs
- 2 cups milk
- 2 cups cooked rice
- 2 cups cheese
- Parmesan cheese
- 2 cups cooked broccoli

DIRECTIONS

1. In a bowl place broccoli and microwave for 2-3 minutes
2. In a pan brown chicken and onion and set aside
3. Mix all ingredients and place in a casserole dish

4. Sprinkle with parmesan cheese and bake for 60 minutes at 375 F

5. When ready remove and serve

Serves: *12*
Prep Time: *10*   Minutes

Cook Time: *50*   Minutes

Total Time: *60*   Minutes

INGREDIENTS

- 1 cup flour
- 1 cup oats
- 1 tsp cinnamon
- 1 cup sugar
- 1 stick unsalted butter
- 2 cups blueberries
- 2 tablespoons cornstarch
- 1 cup water

DIRECTIONS

1. In a bowl combine oats, flour, cinnamon, butter and sugar
2. Press oat mixture into a pan
3. Toss the blueberries with lemon zest and place them in the pan

4. Combine sugar and cornstarch and stir in water
5. Place mixture in a pan and boil on low heat
6. Pour cornstarch mixture over the blueberries
7. Bake for 40-50 minutes at 375 F
8. When ready remove and serve

Serves: 2
Prep Time: 5   Minutes

Cook Time: 15   Minutes

Total Time: 20   Minutes

INGREDIENTS

- 2 cups brussels sprouts
- 1 tablespoon olive oil
- 2 tablespoons parmesan cheese
- ¼ cup fruit vinegar

DIRECTIONS

1. Cut sprouts in half
2. Toss sprouts with olive oil
3. Roast for 10-12 minutes at 475 F
4. When ready remove from oven and sprinkle parmesan cheese and fruit vinegar

Serves: **4**

Prep Time: **10** Minutes

Cook Time: **90** Minutes

Total Time: **100** Minutes

INGREDIENTS

- 2 cups black-eyed peas
- 2 cups water
- 4 cloves garlic
- 1 cup celery
- ¼ tsp diced
- ¼ tsp thyme
- ¼ tsp ginger
- ¼ tsp curry powder
- ¼ tsp black pepper

DIRECTIONS

1. In a pot add black-eyed peas, vegetables, seasoning and bring to boil
2. Cover and cook until tender for 90 minutes
3. When ready remove from heat and serve

Serves: *8*

Prep Time: *10*   Minutes

Cook Time: *20*   Minutes

Total Time: *30*   Minutes

INGREDIENTS

- 1 lb. ground beef
- ¼ cup onion
- 1 tsp cumin
- ¼ tsp black pepper
- 1 garlic clove
- 8 corn tortillas
- 1 can enchilada sauce

DIRECTIONS

1. In a pan fry meat, add garlic, cumin, pepper, onion and cook until onion is soft
2. In another pan fry tortillas
3. Dip each tortilla in enchilada sauce and fill with meat mixture

4. Place enchilada in a pan and top with sauce and cheese

5. Bake enchiladas at 350 F for 20 minutes or until golden brown

Serves: *8*
Prep Time: *5*   Minutes

Cook Time: *20*   Minutes

Total Time: *25*   Minutes

INGREDIENTS

- 8 eggs
- ¼ cup mayonnaise
- 1 tsp mustard
- paprika

DIRECTIONS

1. Place eggs in a pot and bring to a boil
2. Boil the eggs for about 12-15 minutes
3. Cut boiled eggs in half
4. Remove the yolks
5. Mix mayonnaise, mustard and yolks together
6. Spoon mixture into each white and sprinkle with paprika
7. Serve when ready

Serves: **2**

Prep Time: **10** Minutes

Cook Time: **95** Minutes

Total Time: **105** Minutes

INGREDIENTS

- 1 tablespoon black pepper
- 2 lbs. beef stew
- ¼ cup vegetable oil
- ¼ cup mushrooms
- 1 carrot
- ¼ tsp garlic
- ¼ tsp dried thyme
- 1 can chicken broth
- 2 cups water
- 1 package vegetables
- 2 potatoes
- ¼ cup barley

DIRECTIONS

1. In a pot heat oil and sauté stew for 5-6 minutes
2. Add onions, mushrooms, carrots and sauté for another 3-4 minutes
3. Add thyme, garlic, broth, mixed vegetables, barley, and potatoes
4. Stir and stir to boil
5. Cover, reduce heat and simmer for 90 minutes
6. When ready remove from heat and serve

Serves: **6**

Prep Time: **5**   Minutes

Cook Time: **15** Minutes

Total Time: **20** Minutes

INGREDIENTS

- 1 butternut squash
- 1 tablespoon olive oil
- 1 tablespoon brown sugar
- 1 tablespoon butter

DIRECTIONS

1. Brush squash with olive oil and grill for 5-10 minutes
2. When tender brush with melted butter and sugar
3. Grill for another 2-3 minutes
4. When ready remove and serve

Serves: *1*
Prep Time: **5**   Minutes

Cook Time: **5**   Minutes

Total Time: **10** Minutes

INGREDIENTS

- 1 tablespoon wheat germ
- 1 tsp vanilla extract
- 1 banana
- ½ cup low-fat milk
- ¼ cup cooked oatmeal
- ¼ tsp brown sugar

DIRECTIONS

1. **In a blender add all ingredients and blend until smooth**
2. **Pour the smoothie in a glass and serve**

Serves: **6**

Prep Time: **10**   Minutes

Cook Time: **20**   Minutes

Total Time: **30**   Minutes

INGREDIENTS

- 1 potato
- ¼ cup flour
- 2 cup low-fat milk
- 2 oz. cheese
- ¼ cup fat-free sour cream

DIRECTIONS

1. Cut baked potatoes into cubes
2. In a saucepan add flour, milk and stir well
3. Add potato and cook on low heat
4. Add cheese and cook until cheese is fully melted
5. Remove from heat, stir in sour cream and mix well
6. Serve when ready

Serves: **2**
Prep Time: **10**   Minutes

Cook Time: **45**   Minutes

Total Time: **55**   Minutes

INGREDIENTS

- 1 acorn squash
- 1 tsp unsalted butter
- 1 tsp brown sugar
- 2 tablespoon pineapple
- ¼ tsp nutmeg

DIRECTIONS

1. In a baking pan place squash, add butter, sugar and acorn half
2. Cover squash and bake for 25-30 minutes at 425 F
3. Scoop cooked squash
4. Combine cooked squash, butter, nutmeg, pineapple and spoon mixture into shell
5. Bake for another 12-15 minutes at 450F
6. When ready remove from heat and serve

PASTA

Serves: **3**

Prep Time: **10** Minutes

Cook Time: **20** Minutes

Total Time: **30** Minutes

INGREDIENTS

- 1 cup nettle leaves
- ½ cup parmesan cheese
- ½ cup olive oil
- 10 oz. pasta
- 3 garlic cloves
- ½ cup walnuts

DIRECTIONS

1. In a food processor add garlic, walnuts, and leaves
2. Blend until smooth and olive oil and stir in parmesan cheese
3. Cook pasta and drain it
4. Sit in nettle pesto

5. Transfer onto serving plates and garnish with salt

Serves: **4**

Prep Time: **10**   Minutes

Cook Time: **30**   Minutes

Total Time: **40**   Minutes

INGREDIENTS

- 2 cups butternut squash
- 1 tablespoon olive oil
- 2 pieces of bacon
- 2 chicken breasts
- ¼ coconut cream
- 1 tablespoon apple cider vinegar
- 1 tablespoon coconut oil
- 1 tsp salt
- 1 tsp garlic powder
- 1 zucchini

DIRECTIONS

1. Spiralize the zucchini into noodles and cook in olive oil

2. In a blender add coconut cream, coconut oil, squash, vinegar, salt, garlic powder and blend until smooth

3. Pour the mixture over the noodles and toss to coat

4. Serve when ready

Serves:	**4**
Prep Time:	**10** Minutes
Cook Time:	**2h 50** Minutes
Total Time:	**3h** Minutes

INGREDIENTS

- 1-pound lean beef
- ¼ cup onion
- 3 cloves garlic
- 2 cans tomatoes
- 1 6-ounces can tomato paste
- 2 anchovy fillets
- 1 tsp oregano
- ½ tsp red pepper
- 6-ounces penne pasta
- 1/3 cup olives
- ½ cup parsley

DIRECTIONS

1. In a skillet add onion, garlic, and beef and cook on medium heat
2. In a slow cooker combine the beef mixture with anchovies, oregano, tomato paste, and red pepper
3. Cook for 5-6 hours
4. When ready, stir olives and parsley in the cooker
5. When ready remove and serve with parsley

MORNING SALAD

Serves: **2**

Prep Time: **5**   Minutes

Cook Time: **5**   Minutes

Total Time: **10**   Minutes

INGREDIENTS

- 1 onion
- 1 tsp cumin
- 1 tablespoon olive oil
- 1 avocado
- ¼ lb. cooked lentils
- 1 oz. walnuts
- Coriander
- ¼ lb. feta cheese
- Salad dressing of choice
- 8-10 baby carrots

DIRECTIONS

1. In a bowl combine all ingredients together and mix well
2. Add dressing and serve

Serves: *2*

Prep Time: *5*   Minutes

Cook Time: *5*   Minutes

Total Time: *10* Minutes

INGREDIENTS

- 2 cups cooked rice
- 2 cups apples 2 tablespoons sunflower seeds
- 2 tablespoons balsamic vinegar
- 1 tablespoon olive oil
- 1 tsp honey
- 1 tsp mustard
- 1 tsp orange peel

DIRECTIONS

1. In a bowl combine all ingredients together and mix well
2. Add dressing and serve

Serves: **2**
Prep Time: **5** Minutes

Cook Time: **5** Minutes

Total Time: **10** Minutes

INGREDIENTS

- ¼ tsp sugar
- ¼ tsp water
- ½ cup walnuts
- 4 cups leaf lettuce
- 4 Asian pears
- 2 oz. blue cheese
- ¼ cup pomegranate seeds
- Olive oil

DIRECTIONS

1. In a bowl combine all ingredients together and mix well
2. Add dressing and serve

Serves: **2**

Prep Time: **5**   Minutes

Cook Time: **5**   Minutes

Total Time: **10**   Minutes

INGREDIENTS

- 4 beets
- ¼ cup walnuts
- 1 cup leaf lettuce
- ¼ cup basil
- ¼ cup herb vinegar
- 1 tablespoon olive oil
- 2 oz. blue cheese

DIRECTIONS

1. In a bowl combine all ingredients together and mix well
2. Add dressing and serve

Serves: **2**
Prep Time: **5**   Minutes

Cook Time: **5**   Minutes

Total Time: **10**   Minutes

INGREDIENTS

- 1 cup cooked rice
- 1 cup water
- 1 cup collard greens
- ¼ cup onion
- 2 cups berries
- ¼ cup blueberries
- 1 tablespoon lemon juice
- ¼ cup mint
- 1 tablespoon olive oil

DIRECTIONS

1. In a bowl combine all ingredients together and mix well
2. Add dressing and serve

Serves: **2**

Prep Time: **5** Minutes

Cook Time: **5** Minutes

Total Time: **10** Minutes

INGREDIENTS

- 2 packages ramen noodles
- 2 tablespoons olive oil
- 1 tablespoon sesame seeds
- 1 cup cooked chicken
- ¼ head cabbage
- 2 green onions
- ¼ tablespoon sugar
- 1 tablespoon sesame oil
- ¼ cup wine vinegar

DIRECTIONS

1. In a bowl combine all ingredients together and mix well
2. Add dressing and serve

Serves: 2

Prep Time: 5   Minutes

Cook Time: 5   Minutes

Total Time: 10   Minutes

INGREDIENTS

- 6 oz. sells pasta
- ¼ cup sour cream
- ¼ cup mayonnaise
- ¼ tsp celery seed
- 1 tsp onion powder
- ¼ tsp mustard
- ¼ cup pickles
- 1 stalks celery

DIRECTIONS

1. In a bowl combine all ingredients together and mix well
2. Add dressing and serve

Serves: **2**

Prep Time: **5**   Minutes

Cook Time: **5**   Minutes

Total Time: **10**   Minutes

INGREDIENTS

- 1 tsp curry powder
- ¼ cup mayonnaise
- 1 cup cooked chicken
- 2 green onions
- 2 celery stalks
- ¼ cup nuts
- ¼ cup raisins

DIRECTIONS

1. In a bowl combine all ingredients together and mix well
2. Add dressing and serve

Serves: **2**

Prep Time: **5**   Minutes

Cook Time: **5**   Minutes

Total Time: **10**   Minutes

INGREDIENTS

- 2 cups chicken breasts
- 1 cup almonds
- 1 stalk celery
- 1 green onion
- 1 cup grapes
- 1 apple
- ¼ cup sour cream
- ¼ cup mayonnaise
- 1 tsp rice vinegar
- ¼ tsp sugar

DIRECTIONS

1. In a bowl combine all ingredients together and mix well
2. Add dressing and serve

Serves: 2

Prep Time: 5   Minutes

Cook Time: 5   Minutes

Total Time: *10*   Minutes

INGREDIENTS

- ¼ cup red wine vinegar
- 1 tablespoon mustard
- ¼ cup olive oil
- 1 head romaine lettuce
- 2 hard-boiled eggs
- 8 oz. cooked chicken
- 4 slices bacon
- 1 avocado
- 2 oz. blue cheese
- 4 oz. cherry tomatoes

DIRECTIONS

1. In a bowl combine all ingredients together and mix well
2. Add dressing and serve

Serves: 2

Prep Time: 5   Minutes

Cook Time: 5   Minutes

Total Time: 10   Minutes

INGREDIENTS

- 1 head cauliflower
- ¼ sour cream
- ½ cup mayonnaise
- 1 tablespoon lemon juice
- 1 tablespoon garlic powder
- 1 cup cheddar cheese
- ¼ cup chives

DIRECTIONS

1. In a bowl combine all ingredients together and mix well
2. Add dressing and serve

THANK YOU FOR READING THIS BOOK!

Made in the USA
Las Vegas, NV
23 April 2021